Mickey's Found Sounds
A Musical Exploration Storybook

EXPLORE MUSIC

Explore an interactive experience online! Go to:
www.halleonard.com/exploremusic/00160409

Printed in the United States of America

ISBN 978-1-4950-6478-4

Published by Hal Leonard LLC
7777 W. Bluemound Road
P.O. Box 13819
Milwaukee, WI 53213

Contents

Mickey Mouse looked out his window on the morning of the town parade. "What a beautiful day," he exclaimed.

"This is a perfect day for a parade! I'm going to call my friends and invite them to come with me!"

Soon Minnie, Donald, Daisy, and Goofy arrived.

"The parade will need marchers," Mickey said.

"Great idea, Mickey!" said Daisy. "What will we do?"

"I made a list," said Minnie, "We could carry balloons or ride bicycles!"

"We could decorate a
fire engine or make a float,"
said Donald.

"We could twirl lassos," said Goofy.

"Those are all great ideas!" said Mickey.
"Let's get going!"

"You bet," said Goofy.

They didn't want to get hungry while they were at the parade, so they packed a picnic lunch and jumped in the car to drive to the parade grounds.

But just when they got there, it started to rain.

"Oh dear," cried Minnie, "Now we're getting all wet!
And the parade is going to be cancelled!"

They rushed to the car and no one said a word all the way home. Mickey could tell that his friends were disappointed about the parade.

As they walked into the house, Mickey got an idea. "I know," he said, "Since the parade was cancelled, let's have our own parade inside the house. We can even have a marching band!"

"But, Mickey," exclaimed Minnie, "We don't have any instruments."

Mickey replied, "Let's look around and see what we can find that can make sounds. It will be easy and fun!"

Turn the page to see what they found!

Empty Oatmeal Container

Plastic Bucket

Hole Punch

Wooden Spoons

Clear Tape

Construction Paper

Markers

17

Empty Plastic Bottles

Beans

Rubber Bands

Cardboard Tube

Wax Paper

Pencils

Glass Jars

Go to the next page to see what Mickey and his friends made!

(Ask an adult to help you with these activities.)

Materials

- Plastic bucket
- Two wooden spoons

 Turn the bucket upside down and use two wooden spoons for drumsticks.

Play

Play with two sticks at a time, or alternate sticks left and right.

Go online for more activities
www.halleonard.com/exploremusic/00160409

OATMEAL CONGA DRUM

Materials

- Markers
- Empty oatmeal container (the big size is best)
- Construction paper to fit around the container
- Clear tape

 1 Use your markers to make your own colorful picture on a big sheet of paper.

 **2** Tape the lid closed.

3 Tape the paper around the container.

Play
Use the tips of your fingers to play the drum. Play with both hands, or alternate left and right.

PLASTIC BOTTLE SHAKER

Materials

- Medium size plastic bottle
- Dry beans (or quinoa or rice)
- Construction paper to fit around the container
- Markers
- Clear tape

1 Place the beans (or quinoa or rice) inside the bottle and replace the cap. Experiment with the amount to see what sounds best to you.

2 Use your markers to create a colorful design on the construction paper.

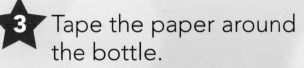 Tape the paper around the bottle.

Play
Shake the bottle to make a sound.

TUBE KAZOO

Materials

- Wax paper
- Cardboard tube
- Rubber band
- Hole punch

 Punch a hole in one end of the cardboard tube.

 Place wax paper on the opposite end.

 Place a rubber band *tightly* around the wax paper to hold the wax paper in place.

4 Place the tube over your mouth and sing the word "doo." Be careful not to cover the hole you punched!

Play

You can play anything you can sing. Sing "Mary Had a Little Lamb" or "Twinkle, Twinkle Little Star" with the word "doo."

GLASS JAR XYLOPHONE

Materials

- Glass jars
- Pencils (or wooden chopsticks)
- Water

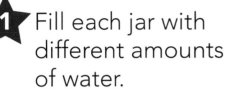 **1** Fill each jar with different amounts of water.

2 Tap each jar gently with a pencil to hear the highness or lowness of the sound being played.

3 What happens when you add more water?

4 What happens when you remove water?

5 Experiment with different amounts of water until you find sounds that you like.

Play

Place the jars in a line from the lowest sounds on the left to the highest sounds on the right. Tap each jar gently with a pencil to play a melody.

"Hooray!" everyone shouted. "We have a band of found sounds!"

Now you can play along with Mickey and the band!

LOOK WHAT WE FOUND!

Lookin' around can be an adventure.

Just lookin' around can be lots of fun.

You never know what you'll find; it could be one of a kind.

And when you find it, the fun has just begun!

Hey, look what we found, just by lookin' around.

Lookin' left, right, up, and down.

Hey, look what we found, just by lookin' around.

Now it's time for us to find out:

Just how does it sound?

Now, it goes . . .

Let's drum!
Ka-boom, boom, pow!

Shake it up!

Shake-a-shake-a-shake-a-shake shake!

Kazoo!

Doot doo doo doot doot doo doo!

Now let's all play!

Sing along online
www.halleonard.com/exploremusic/00160409

Message to Parents & Caregivers

Young children learn through play and hands-on activities. Often this involves the use of toys, puppets, or other tactile items. Homemade musical instruments provide a fun and unique opportunity to introduce children to music and the arts.

Many percussion instruments can be easily made at home using everyday items. *Mickey's Found Sounds* shows how to make a variety of percussion instruments that children love to play. Take a few minutes to help your child gather the needed materials. Then, enjoy some creative time together making the instruments and playing them for friends and family.

Playing music instruments helps children grasp musical concepts and develop cognitive skills. It also gives children the opportunity to:

- explore sounds of different instruments
- develop gross and fine motor skills
- encourage imaginative play
- understand where sound comes from and how it changes
- learn about different cultures

Children love to play drums, shake shakers, and make melodies of their own. Exploring and experimenting with the different sounds of homemade instruments will inspire children to make their own music and express themselves in their own unique and wonderful way!

Access online content:
www.halleonard.com/exploremusic/00160409